Dear Parents and Educators,

Welcome to Penguin Young Readers! As parents and educators, you know that each child develops at their own pace—in terms of speech, critical thinking, and, of course, reading. Penguin Young Readers recognizes this fact. As a result, each Penguin Young Readers book is assigned a traditional easy-to-read level (1–4) as well as an F&P Text Level (A–P). Both of these systems will help you choose the right book for your child. Please refer to the back of each book for specific leveling information. Penguin Young Readers features esteemed authors and illustrators, stories about favorite characters, fascinating nonfiction, and more!

Xavier Riddle and the Secret Museum: I am Eleanor Roosevelt	LEVEL **3**
	F&P TEXT LEVEL **M**

This book is perfect for a **Transitional Reader** who:
- can read multisyllable and compound words;
- can read words with prefixes and suffixes;
- is able to identify story elements (beginning, middle, end, plot, setting, characters, problem, solution); and
- can understand different points of view.

Here are some **activities** you can do during and after reading this book:
- Research: Eleanor Roosevelt was the First Lady of the United States when her husband was the President. Go to the library or use the internet to learn about other First Ladies.
- Creative Writing: Pretend you got a job at the Secret Museum! Write a journal entry about that day. How did you feel? What was your job? Were you nervous or excited? Describe your day.

Remember, sharing the love of reading with a child is the best gift you can give!

*This book has been officially leveled by using the F&P Text Level Gradient™ leveling system.

PENGUIN YOUNG READERS

An Imprint of Penguin Random House LLC, New York

Penguin supports copyright. Copyright fuels creativity, encourages diverse voices,
promotes free speech, and creates a vibrant culture. Thank you for buying an authorized
edition of this book and for complying with copyright laws by not reproducing, scanning,
or distributing any part of it in any form without permission. You are supporting writers
and allowing Penguin to continue to publish books for every reader.

Published in 2020 by Penguin Young Readers, an imprint of Penguin Random House LLC, New York.
Manufactured in China.

Visit us online at www.penguinrandomhouse.com.

ISBN 9780593096345 (pbk)   10 9 8 7 6 5 4 3 2 1
ISBN 9780593096413 (hc)   10 9 8 7 6 5 4 3 2 1

I am Eleanor Roosevelt

adapted by Brooke Vitale

It is job day at the museum.
Xavier, Yadina, and Brad spin
a wheel to pick their jobs.

Yadina is a tour guide.

Brad is in charge of the snack stand.

"I am a map hander-outer?" Xavier asks. "Boring!"

"I want to do something *big*,"
Xavier says.

"To the Secret Museum!"
Yadina says.

They wonder *who* they will meet.

They wonder *where* they will go.

They wonder *when* they will go.

They find a microphone!

They wonder whose it was.

The microphone belonged
to Eleanor Roosevelt.

"I wonder if she can help me
get a better job," Xavier says.

The friends put their hands on
Berby.

They travel back in time
to New York in 1902.

They land in front of a hotel.

"What's going on in there?"

Yadina asks.

"A fancy party," a voice answers.

The friends turn around.

They see Eleanor Roosevelt.

"A fancy party?" Yadina asks.
"Why are you out here then?"
Eleanor would rather help people
than dance at a party.

"That's like me," Xavier says.
"I'd rather do *anything* than
be a map hander-outer."

Eleanor sees a small boy looking through the hotel window.

He seems sad.

"I see a chance to do something helpful right now," Eleanor says.

She asks the boy if he wants
to learn how to dance.

He nods.

"Can we learn, too?" Yadina asks.

Eleanor smiles. "Of course!
Follow me."

The friends are having so much fun.

"This is wonderful," the boy says.

But Xavier is not sure how dancing
will solve his problem.

"Should I do a dance while
I hand out maps?" he asks.

Yadina points at Berby. "Hang on. We're about to find out!"

This time the friends travel
to the White House.

"Welcome to the White House!"

Eleanor Roosevelt says.

She tells the friends that
she is now the First Lady.

That means she is married
to the President.

"What does the First Lady do?" Xavier asks.

As First Lady, Eleanor takes every chance to help others.

She visits hurt soldiers.

She helps children.

She fights for what is right.

Just then, Eleanor sees the clock.

It is time for her radio show.

"Want to watch?" she asks.

Yadina, Xavier, and Brad watch
as Eleanor starts her show.

"Look!" Xavier says. "It's the
microphone from the Secret
Museum!"

"She is using her job to help others," Xavier says. "Maybe my job at the museum is a chance to help others, too."

Back at the museum, Xavier
helps people use their maps
to find their favorite things.